ART
MASTERPIECES

AFTER

BY **WARD KIMBALL**

MAGNUM BOOKS
Methuen Paperbacks Ltd.

A MAGNUM BOOK

ART AFTERPIECES

ISBN: 0 417 05790 3

Published in the United States of America by
Price/Stern/Sloan Publishers, Inc., 410 North La Cienega Boulevard,
Los Angeles, California 90048

Published in Great Britain 1979 by Magnum Books

Copyright © 1964, 1975 by Ward Kimball

Magnum Books are published by Methuen Paperbacks Ltd.,
11 New Fetter Lane, London EC4P 4EE

Printed in the United States of America

ART AFTERPIECES

MONA LISA

LEONARDO DA VINCI

1452 · 1519

INTRODUCTION

People have unquestionably one really effective weapon — laughter.

I wish I'd said this, but Mark Twain beat me to it.

And speaking of laughter, here is a funny art book by Ward Kimball, who worked at Disney's for many years as a director and producer. He and I had a lot of fun doing one of those "Mouse Factory" TV shows. I'm sorry we couldn't do 100 of them together.

Now, as I look back, I realize that we all are still working in a "Mouse Factory," and along with the peanut butter and jelly sandwich, we have a thermos of diet root beer and our hard-boiled egg with a Mickey Mouse on it. Right, Ward? (I wrote that.)

Good luck with your book, Ward. One of the best ways to sell a million copies is to sit in a bookstore window dressed as Frankenstein's make-up man.

Jonathan Winters

PORTRAIT OF MY MOTHER
(Arrangement in Black and Gray)

JAMES McNEILL WHISTLER

1834 · 1903

CREATION OF ADAM

MICHELANGELO

1475 · 1564

PORTRAIT OF A MAN WITH A MEDAL

SANDRO BOTTICELLI

1444? · 1510

DIANA

FRANCOIS BOUCHER

1703 · 1770

THE BLUE BOY

THOMAS GAINSBOROUGH

1727 · 1788

THE DRAWBRIDGE

VINCENT VAN GOGH

1853 · 1890

THE MONEYLENDER AND HIS WIFE

QUENTIN MASSYS

1466? · 1530

THE ARTIST IN HIS STUDIO

JAN VERMEER

1632 · 1675

THE AVENUE

MEINDERT HOBBEMA

1638 · 1709

IN THE BOAT

EDOUARD MANET

1832 · 1883

THE BIRTH OF VENUS

SANDRO BOTTICELLI

1444? · 1510

COUNT DUKE OF OLIVARES

DIEGO VELAZQUEZ

1599 · 1660

ALLEGORY

(Alfonso d'Este and Laura Diante)

TITIAN

1477 · 1576

VENUS AND CUPID

DIEGO VELAZQUEZ

1599 · 1660

LUNCHEON ON THE GRASS

EDOUARD MANET

1832 · 1883

THE FIGHT FOR THE WATER HOLE

FREDERIC REMINGTON

1861 · 1909

THE ABDUCTION OF
THE DAUGHTERS OF LEUCIPPUS

PETER PAUL RUBENS

1577 · 1640

ARISTOTLE WITH BUST

REMBRANDT

1606 · 1669

LE MEZZETIN

JEAN ANTOINE WATTEAU

1684 · 1721

THE SMOKERS

ADRIAEN BROUWER

1605 · 1638

CRISPIN AND SCAPIN

HONORE DAUMIER

1808 · 1879

THE SHADY GROVE

JEAN HONORE FRAGONARD

1732 · 1806

AN OLD MAN AND HIS GRANDSON

GHIRLANDAIO

1449 · 1494

THE CHASTISEMENT OF LOVE

SCHOOL OF CARAVAGGIO

1573? · ?1610

NUDE FIXING HER HAIR

EDGAR DEGAS

1834 · 1917

THE ABDUCTION OF THE SABINE WOMEN

NICOLAS POUSSIN

1594 · 1665

PORTRAIT OF NICCOLO SPINELLI

HANS MEMLING

1430? · 1495

ST. LUKE DRAWING THE VIRGIN MARY

JAN GOSSAERT

1478? · ?1533

THE ANATOMY LESSON
or
THE ANATOMY OF DR. TULP

REMBRANDT

1606 · 1669

ADAM TEMPTED BY EVE

LUCAS CRANACH THE ELDER

1472 · 1553

THE VISITATION

MARIOTTO ALBERTINELLI

1474 · 1515

PORTRAIT OF ARNAULD D'ANDILLY

PHILIPPE DE CHAMPAIGNE

1602 · 1674

SUNFLOWERS IN A VASE

VINCENT VAN GOGH

1853 · 1890

THE GLEANERS

JEAN FRANCOIS MILLET

1814 · 1875

APELLES PAINTING A PORTRAIT OF CAMPASPE

GIOVANNI TIEPOLO

1696 · 1770

THE OLD BRIDGE

HUBERT ROBERT

1733 · 1808

SEPTEMBER MORN

PAUL CHABAS

1869 · 1937

PINKIE

SIR THOMAS LAWRENCE

1769 · 1830

HELENE FOURMENT

PETER PAUL RUBENS

1577 · 1640

PORTRAIT OF A LADY

ROGIER VAN DER WEYDEN

1399? · 1464

GEORGE WASHINGTON

GILBERT STUART

1755 · 1828

THE WHITE GIRL

JAMES McNEILL WHISTLER

1834 · 1903

THE BATTLE OF THE ROMANS AND SABINES

JACQUES-LOUIS DAVID

1748 · 1824

MOUNTED OFFICER OF THE IMPERIAL GUARD

THEODORE GERICAULT

1791 · 1824

MAGNUM

Ward Kimball has been involved with art since the age of three, when he drew his first picture of a railroad train. He went to work for Walt Disney at the age of 20 and for the next 39 years was involved in every creative aspect of the Disney output — from cartoons to Disneyland — as an animator and producer.

In 1950, with a group of Disney artists, he organized the now famous Dixieland band, the Firehouse Five Plus Two.

He retired in 1973 to devote more time to his lifelong hobby, railroads. He operates his own railroad museum of historical old equipment, including three full-size locomotives. He also exhibits his kinetic paintings in group and one-man shows in California, and teaches classes in film graphics.

Art Afterpieces is the fulfillment of a small boy's dream — from painting moustaches on ladies' faces in advertisements — to "improving" the world's great masterpieces. In Ward Kimball's case, the dream came true.